TO THE HOPS + THE

HAPPY CHRISTMAS + ...

WITH LOTS OF LOVE

CATHY + PETER

CHRISTMAS 2013

SKY HIGH
SOUTH
CORNWALL COAST

PHOTOGRAPHY BY JASON HAWKES

First published in Great Britain in 2009

Photographs © 2009 Jason Hawkes

British Library Cataloguing-in-Publication Data
A CIP record for this title is available from the British Library

ISBN 978 1 906887 50 6

PiXZ Books
Halsgrove House, Ryelands Industrial Estate,
Bagley Road, Wellington, Somerset TA21 9PZ
Tel: 01823 653777
Fax: 01823 216796
email: sales@halsgrove.com

An imprint of Halstar Ltd, part of the Halsgrove group of companies
Information on all Halsgrove titles is available at: www.halsgrove.com

Printed and bound by Grafiche Flaminia, Italy

Introduction

Through these superb photographs we are taken on an aerial journey along South Cornwall's coast, starting at Land's End and heading eastward for around 80 miles or so (130km) to the Devon border. The delight of this book is that is offers the reader a chance to see just how varied is the southern coast of Cornwall. From the soaring cliffs around the Lizard, we travel east looking down on sandy coves and hidden tidal creeks and into the heart of the many coastal towns and villages along the way.

These days, the coastline provides the means for thousands to enjoy leisure pursuits. The South West Coast Path follows the cliff edge for most of its route through Cornwall, while golden beaches are thronged in summer months providing safe bathing, in most places, while easy access gives everyone a chance to explore harbourside towns and villages.

Jason Hawkes is one of the country's best-known photographers specialising in aerial photography. This little book is the perfect memento for those who wish to take a little bit of Cornwall home with them.

Rugged sea-worn cliffs at Land's End.

Mousehole harbour.

Left: Minack Theatre. Productions first began here in the 1930s.

The heart of Newlyn.

Right: Mount's Bay and Penzance.

St Michael's Mount looking towards Marazion.

Right: Prussia Cove.

Praa Sands has long been one of Cornwall's premier tourist areas. Hoe Point stands in the foreground.

Overleaf:
The harbour, Porthleven.

Mullion Cove lies on the west side of the Lizard peninsula.

Kynance Cove.

A dramatic view over Dinas Cove and Black Head, looking towards Coverack.

Left: An assortment of boats line up on the shore at Cadgwith Cove.

The harbour wall, Coverack.

Overleaf:
Alone at last!

Helford village (foreground) looking over the Helford River with Porthnavas Creek on the left.

Gillan and Flushing stand on the right at the head of the Helford River on Gillan Creek. The church of St Anthony-in-Meneague can be seen on the left bank.

A spectacular view over
Falmouth Harbour,
Gyllyngvase Beach on the left.

Pendennis Castle was built by Henry VIII to guard Falmouth Harbour.

Right: Overlooking the Penryn River towards Falmouth and the sea.

The Fal River with Feock on the left.

Left: The view over Carrick Roads from Mylor Churchtown, St Just in Roseland beyond.

Looking inland over the Carrick Roads towards Truro.

Left: Restronguet Point.

St Anthony Head, with Falmouth on the far side of the Currick Roads.

Towan Beach, St Mawes beyond.

Right: Strolling on the shore.

East Portholland.

Left: Nare Head looking towards Porthscatho and Gerrans.

Hemmick Beach below Boswinger.

The delightful little harbour at Gorran Haven.

Chapel Point with Portmellon in the distance.

Mevagissey.

Looking over Porthpean with St Austell inland.

Right: The harbour at Par.

Gribbin Head stands at the eastern side of St Austell Bay.

Looking upriver at Fowey.

Looking back towards
St Austell Bay with Polruan
(left) and Fowey in sunlight
on the far side of the river.

The Quay at Polruan.

Left: From Fowey looking into Polruan.

Looking down on to the old blockhouse on the Polruan shore of the Fowey river.

Right: East and West Looe, looking out to sea.

East Looe and the
famous Banjo Pier.

Looe Island.

Left: The road bridge crossing the River Looe.

Downderry, east of Looe.

Overleaf:
Endless summer.

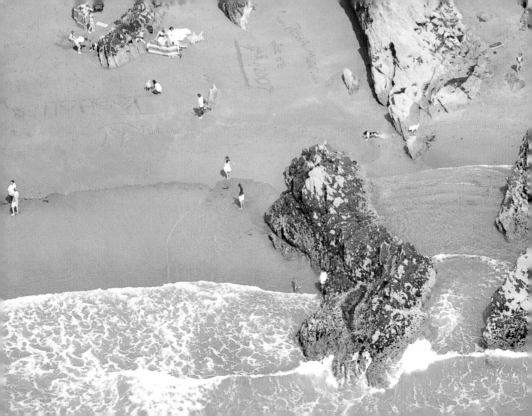

Kingsand.

Left: Kitesurfers at Longsands Beach near Portwrinkle.

The lighthouse on Plymouth Breakwater.